Copyright © 2020 Rakesh Lalchandani

All rights reserved

The characters and events portrayed in this book are fictitious. Any similarity to real persons, living or dead, is coincidental and not intended by the author.

No part of this book may be reproduced, or stored in a retrieval system, or transmitted in any form or by any means, electronic, mechanical, photocopying, recording, or otherwise, without express written permission of the publishe

ISBN: 9798650081777

Cover design by: Art Painter
Library of Congress Control Number: 2018675309
Printed in the United States of America

*I dedicate this book to my wife, Shivika, and my daughter Mohika
for their endless belief in me.
I also dedicate this book to everyone who aims to make
it big in this wonderful profession of selling.*

Sales is an outcome, not a goal. Its a function of doing numerous things right, starting from the moment you target a potential prospect untill you finalize the deal.

JILL KONARTH

CONTENTS

INTRODUCTION

"55% of the people making their living in sales don't have the right skill sets to be successful."

This is a substantial claim made by stalwarts in the industry and the reason this research holds is that salespeople have stopped investing in upgrading their selling skills,

The way consumers buy is changing rapidly; therefore, it becomes necessary to regularly revisit our selling process.

Another statistic states *that 20% of salespeople account for 80% of sales,* the question is that could this happen by luck? I do not think so; Successful salespeople operate in a structured manner; they practice a set structure of selling repeatedly.

This book is based on the good practices followed by successful salespeople, that set them apart from the others, I have learned these principals by observing dynamic salespeople in action throughout my 10 + years of corporate sales career.

This book is useful for everyone looking to make a living by selling. Everyone considering selling as a profession or someone who is already an established salesperson, can use it to upgrade their selling skills,

Over the years, I worked with many sales superstars, and what's interesting is to observe that successful salespeople had common patterns/ habits when it came to selling. By following these habits, I grew exponentially in my field, and today through this book, I am sharing with you the things that I have learned. I hope you enjoy it.

Using these principals, I have been able to get in more clients, make more money, grew almost at a phenomenal scale; you can start increasing your numbers too and add a catalyst to your career.

Use this book as a practical guide to your sales calls also selling concepts are explained with examples for quick understanding. I thank you and appreciate your decision to buy this book and invest in yourself.

PREFACE

Ten years ago after completing my MBA in Marketing, I got recruited by a hospitality firm, to sell their rooms and banquets, neither was I a hotel management degree holder nor was I a pro at selling, so immediately after joining this firm I was given a three months of training on hotels function,

Post my training I was sent on the field to visit corporate to put their guest in our hotel beds, within the first month of my job I realized that getting into sales may not be the best decision for me, as I felt that I am not cut out for this profession, I guess by that time many of my colleagues started thinking the same about me, so in next three months I was given non-field sales related work,

By then I had made up mind to pursue another profession, so one evening I went on to have a candid conversation with my boss and explained all my vulnerabilities about the selling world,

After a lengthy discussion, he felt that selling would be a more appropriate profession for me. He asked me if I were willing to give it another shot, he was ready to allocate a mentor to help me. I agreed that I was assigned a mentor from the team that evening, my responsibility was to observe and learn from him,

My mentor was a sales champion of the group, he always met his budgets and for obvious reasons he was the blue-eyed boy of many in the company,

During my shadowing phase with him, I learned many new things about selling. Over the years, I worked with many such sales superstars, and what's interesting is to observe that successful

salespeople had common patterns/ habits when it came to selling. By following these habits, I grew exponentially in my field, and today through this book, I am sharing with you the things that I have learned. I hope you enjoy it.
Using these principals, I have been able to get in more clients, make more money, grew almost at a phenomenal scale; you can start increasing your numbers too and add a catalyst to your career.

SALES – THE PROFESSION

*David Ogilvy, (one of the fathers) of modern advertising, once said **"We sell or else,"***

In my understanding, this line implies that we all are in business because we sell, and a statement like this coming for an advertising guru means a lot, what's more, interesting is that technology, digital marketing and electronic commerce, **has still not been able to replicate the impact of direct face to face selling**

Some people consider selling to be pushing people to buy something they do not want, don't need, or can't afford.", in all honesty, selling is much more than that.

Selling is also not about wearing suits and running around the market place, putting undue pressure on the buyer, or talking relentlessly about the product features, desperately hoping that our buyer will take the product on our sheer effort of speaking about it.

Then what is selling – The most compelling definition I came across was the one written by Scott Edinger, **"Selling is moving somebody else to act,"**

An ideal seller's objective is to work with the client and drive a solution towards a persistent problem he is facing,

When you think about the best sales interactions you have had in your life, it will remind you of incidents when a salesperson took a genuine interest in understanding your problem and then attempting to solve it "

"83% of business buyers want salespeople focused on helping them achieve their company goals. (Salesforce)"

"You can get anything you want if you help enough other people get what they want. (Zig Ziglar)"

➤ The foremost revenue generator for any business is the sales division, of which 20 % of the salespeople deliver 80% of the revenues worldwide,

➤ Developing selling skills sets you on a fast growth track in any company,

➤ Commission sales till today is known to be as one of the highest money-making profession in the world.

It takes the right mindset, and the right skill set to be successful in sales, in the upcoming chapter let us explore the 3P's of a successful mindset of a sale's successful salesperson.

A SALES MINDSET

3Ps to flex your sales mulscle

P erseverance

"Perseverance is the hard work you do after you get tired of doing the hard work you already did."

--Newt Gingrich (1943-), American politician, historian, and author

Károly Takács- a tale of perseverance

Károly Takács, a sergeant in the Hungarian army, was a world-class pistol shooter. His single-minded focus was to win an Olympic gold in Pistol shooting. Here are a series of events that unfold that keep him away from winning the medal,

1936 - The Hungarian shooting team denied Karoly for the 1936 Summer Olympics because he was a sergeant, and only commissioned officers were allowed to compete. Now, he had to wait for four more years to participate in the Olympics,

Not losing hope, he continued practicing as he was only 26 and could participate in the next Olympics,

Unfortunately, in 1938, two years before Tokyo Olympic, his right hand was severely injured due to an explosion of a faulty grenade at the army training camp. His wound was so severe that he could never shoot again with the right hand.

His handicap did not stop him to everyone surprise with and indomitable will he started practicing with his left hand,

He even made headlines when he participated and won the UIT World Shooting championship with his left arm rifle shooting, establishing himself as a strong contender for the 1940 Olympics.

Unfortunately games of 1940 were canceled too, he was aging and had to put in more hours of practice to maintain his accuracy, many of close friends advised him to quit the dream of participating in the Olympics, but once again at the age of 34 when ahead full throttle to practice and practiced for the Olympics of 1944

the Olympics of 1944 got canceled to everyone's dismay too, he was mentally broken as he knew that age was catching up, and now, his dream of winning a medal on the world's largest games platform will just stay a dream.

His passion kept him going, and finally, at 38years of age in 1948, he participated in the London Olympics, beating the favorite Argentine Carlos, winning his first Olympic Gold medal.

Keeping his quest alive, he came back in 1952 to win the second gold in Olympics.

Winning 35 national shooting championships, he continually reminds us that Great works are performed not by strength but by perseverance.

"Energy and persistence conquer all things."

– Benjamin Franklin

It is safe to compare a salesperson's life to that of an athlete, try to relate this story to our sales live, and think about how many times we would have changed our goals because things got complicated.

Think about how many times we took rejection personally and decided not to pursue the sale or event how many times have we given up on a client in anticipation of a response.

A recent research states that 80 % of buyers say "no" four times before saying "yes." However, 92 % of sales representatives give up after four negative answers, that means one in 10 salespeople stand to close the deal, what sets them apart is their persistence."

Every successful salesperson has this inbuilt trigger that tells him to go on for one more time when things are not going his way, and that is what makes all the difference.

The good part is that everyone has this trigger mechanism within themselves and can be activated by having a burning desire of what they want and then wholly committing themselves to it.

Successful salespeople build perseverance over time by taking small steps every day. At the end of this segment, I will share with you six personal habits of effective salespeople that help them flex their mental sales muscle.

A Positive Attitude

"Become the person who would attract the results you seek." -Jim Cathcart

I am sure you will agree with me that positive thinking is one of the most remarkable discoveries of humanity. There has already been a lot spoken and written on this subject by western authors and spiritual gurus,

I want to ascertain here that in the field of sales, this one attribute exponentially expedites a salesperson's progress,

Every successful salesperson has it in their DNA to expect a positive outcome. They see the bright side of every situation, which allows them to see many opportunities everywhere.

"The POSITIVE THINKER sees the INVISIBLE, feels the INTANGIBLE, and achieves the IMPOSSIBLE." — Winston Churchill, My Early Life, 1874-1904.

Successful salespeople not only have a positive mindset but a positive attitude.

As per webster, "Attitude" is a mental position regarding a fact or state and

Positive – characterized by affirmation, increase, progression, addition, inclusion, or presence rather than negation, withholding, or absence.

Simply put together, Positive Attitude is a "progressive mental position," the state where you continuously thing positive; you can achieve this mental state with focus and practice.

Traits of successful salespeople

1) They never speak to them (about them), the things they do not want to be true - instead of talking things like I can't achieve this budget, they would always speak stuff like what we can do to make these numbers?

2) They have developed a mental filtration pattern whereby using focus; they continuously see the positives in any given situation; it is like finding a diamond in the mines. The entire focus is only on the diamond and not on the dirt that comes with it.

3) They are aware of their emotions – whenever and external stimuli regards them to look at a darker side of a situation, they again with concentration put their mind consciously to a more uplifting emotion of their mind and do not think dwell or bother about the negative side, they practice this over and over again until it becomes an auto habit.

4) Their awareness is entirely in the present situation; neither do they spend time dwelling on their past performance, nor are they too focused on the future results; their every action is dedicated to making their current progress better.

"The only future lies in action the take to make it happen in the current moment."

5) They surround themselves with like-minded people, **Remember You're the average of the five people spend the most time with,"** - Jim Rohn, successful people make a network of other successful uplifting people who see the good in each other always

If all the elements of sales are the pearls of a necklace, then a positive attitude would be the thread that binds all those elements together. I would not be able to emphasize enough that this is by far the most critical element that sets apart a performing salesperson from an average performer.

P ride
Have you ever come across a salesperson who procrastinates a lot, is regular in taking breaks, and when it comes to performance, he finds himself at the bottom of the pyramid.

Such people need constant supervision to finish a task in time, and they mostly have a negative outlook on any change or new job delegated to them; these are the people who do not take pride in their profession.

You are what you do.

"To be successful, the first thing to do is fall in love with your work- Sister Mary Lauretta"

All successful salespeople have an intense pride and belief in the product they sell and the organization they work for; they have a firm idea that this product is a better fit/solution to people's problems. They can transmit their enthusiasm about the product to the clients,

Your team members, bosses, and clients feel the difference when you take pride in your work.

As per a survey conducted, 64% of salespeople who failed in selling did not fail because they could not sell, but because they were not passionate enough to sell.

Pride builds your self-concept, keeps you motivated, and most importantly, triggers autosuggestions in your brain to focus your awareness back on selling even when the chips are down,

I am not saying that you will always have a perfect product to sell or will have the most supportive operational division or the best value delivered priced product. A salesperson who takes pride in performance will always and always do well even with these handicaps

Following are habits of productive salespeople that help them build the 3P's in their work

Six habits

1) **Success Mapping** – Sales super starts always start by mapping what their success looks like on a mental plane; they visualize what they want an make a concrete goal with a timeline on paper, e.g., I want to make 1cr sales this quarter to earn 3x commission. Once they make the goal, they do not change it no matter what.

2) **They focus on the part, not the whole.** Break a goal into small bite-sized goals, e.g., if I know that I have to achieve 48 lakhs

target every month, I will need to make 2 lakh daily. Now considering a 24day work month, I will further break it down to the number of clients with avg potential businesses required and then plan all daily activities congruent to achieving this bite-sized target.

3) **Prepare big for small** – The idea is to put maximum effort into a niche-defined target rather than spread out energies doing multiple things. To achieve two lakhs a day, a sales manager needs eight accounts with an average spend of 25k per day. Getting these eight onboard looks more achievable and realistic. He now needs to plan and action significantly per account, focusing on closing one report after another.

4) **Do the routine – I fear not the man who has practiced 10,000 kicks once, but I fear the man who has practiced one kick 10,000 times** – Bruce Lee,

Successful salespeople get the routine and boring stuff going no matter what, things like prospecting, updating CRM, doing tele-calls, sending emails, are executed daily.

5) **1% Rule** – Every successful salesperson will always ask himself "if I had to do my every task all over again, what would be that one thing I will do better this time"

They try to improve doing all the small things little by little every day; it's a method of constant improvement in every subject. Whether by writing an email or talking on the phone or doing a price negotiation, or closing deals, they always seek to improve 1% at a time in 1000 different areas continually.

6) **They build an uplifting support network** – things will not always turn out to be as expected, and in such times, losing motivation and interest in a particular task becomes easy. Therefore, successful salespeople build their support network wisely (this network can be one person or a group of people, they can be people from the office close friends or family). Your support network believes in your cause and always see the good in you they

uplift you when you are down, remember Jim Rohn said that we are the average of the five people we spend the most time with, choose your five well.

Japanese Method Of Organization In Selling

"Your input determines your outlook. Your outlook determines your output, and your output determines your future." Zig Ziglar

It is essential to analyze the actions we take (input) in our daily sales lives to have a desired result (output)

In this technology age, I have seen some salespeople spending a lot of time in administrative work; they are piled up with extensive emails and keep participating in activities that are non-revenue generating,

Which sometimes may make them skip doing the essentials such as selling, or filing of the visiting cards in its right space, or arranging marketing collateral in a manner that is easily accessed when required,

Work becomes more faster when you have correct email templates and contract formats, organized client data handy as and when needed.

Therefore, I am presenting to you a Japanese Method of getting lean in you work regular workday.

Its Time To Get Lean

Lean thinking is about changing how you **organize your daily activities** to **enhance work efficiency** while **reducing energy wastage.**

This attribute encourages us to extend Lean Thinking from a shop floor environment to our sales life with the 5S methodology.

What Is 5S?

5S is a Japanese **workplace organization method** achieved by following 5 phases (all which start with "S," both in the original Japanese and in English):

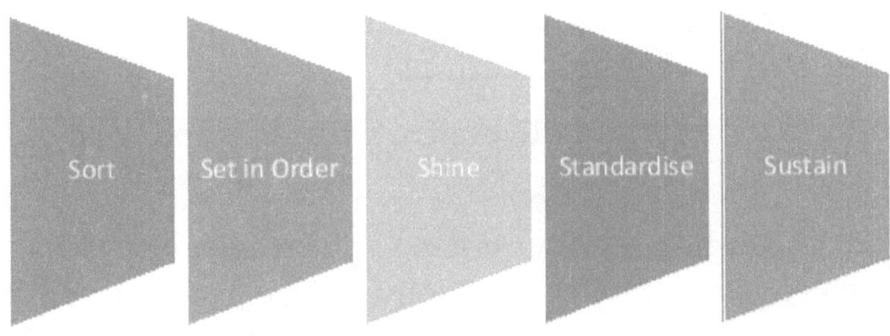

S ort/Seiri
Sorting or segregation is a process based on leaving the unnecessary aside.

The first step for a salesperson is to make an analytical effort to identify what they need and separate it from those things that they feel only take up space. After classifying, the person should throw away everything they do not use.

1) **Database** – check for active and non-active client data, get this data from your CRM or your current company data pool, check for contact/profile changes,

2) **Emails** – Segregate emails into folders for action emails vs. FYI emails and put them in separate folders that have the same con-

tent.

3) **Visiting Cards** – Convert all physical cards to a digital storage and sort them as per usage.

4) **Work Desk** – Always make sure your work desk has limited items which are of current user only. Files, folders, documents need to have a separate space, and kept as per order and usability, as a thumb-rule, **anything not used for long should be discarded** or held in the storage place.

7) **Marketing Collateral** - prearrange your physical and digital marketing collateral in an orderly manner and keep stock of the physical ones. Sort it as per current and old, stay relevant files only, and keep it all in a central location.

9) **Contract Formats** – discard old contract formats and keep up-dated data.

Items that have common attributes need to be "tagged" together. Also, you need to set a timeline for their usage, e.g., if not in use for a year trash them. Sorting out items will help you identify things that you need, but you do not have.

Once you complete the first step successfully, you can prepare for the next stage, choosing the best place for each object.

Set in Order/Seiton

Organization is its main characteristic or Seiton.

Everything you have sorted needs to be **organized as per their importance**, and placed in a **central work area**. The idea is efficient retrieval of recourses when required,

Imagine your workspace/computer/phone as a well-organized wardrobe where you keep workwear, formal wear, accessories, and shoes in different sections.

There are two essential parts to a systematic organization –

a) putting everything in its proper place

b) setting up a system with labeling and identification so that every item is easily retrieved when needed

Once you set everything in order of your need, you are ready to move to the third stage.

S hine/Seiso

Cleanliness is its primary attribute.

In the third stage, a person needs to ensure that the entire facility remains clean always.

You should timely inspect data stored on your phones, email folders, CRM, workspace, and you need to spot irregularities, misalignments, and keep things clean as you go,

You can set aside time as per you convince to do this activity (for example once a week, or every alternate week, etc.),

You also need to take care of your physical workspace and shine/clean elements than just relying on the housekeeping staff to get his done.

Maintenance will help your workspace stay lean; **remember, the more frequently you do this step, the less time it will take to execute this process.**

S tandardize /Seiketsu

A vital attribute of this step is to **avoid deviations**.

In this fourth step, you need to set your system/standards to execute the first three steps on an autopilot.

Once you set everything on order for use, you need to ensure that things do not slide back to the way they were. It would be best if you had standardization of every element to become a part of you live.

This process is about creating regularities, schedules to operate effectively.

Sustain/Shitsuke
Sustainability takes **Self Discipline.**

You can look at constant up-grading in executing things better, testing, and becoming better in your process. Some days you may feel like skipping the whole process and do it the next day, but self-discipline will help you follow your schedule.

Applying the 5S method at work is an excellent way to take control of your space and optimize time.

IDEAL CLIENT PROFILE

Before we plan to reach out to our customers, it is essential to know who our right customers should be.

Ironically, recent studies conducted by Mark Wayshak demonstrated that **50% of prospects are not a good fit for your business.**

Chasing the wrong client builds in more pressure as you run against time on your budgets, you prospect harder and more to make up on time spent on the wrong client. Your sales cycle becomes bigger, building in frustration, making the salesperson more reactive in the process.

The biggest question most salespeople have **is knowing where to hunt** and determining that it becomes instrumental in deciding who your ideal customer should be.

Top salespeople know that it is always good to first have a big fish in the kitty and build a base for midsize clients.

Therefore, they make a plan to define the ideal Client Profile before going after the big fish.

Creating your Ideal client profile

Your Ideal Client Profile is a representation of your best client with whom you would like to work.

With the template mentioned here, you can easily create your ideal client profile; however, getting this right requires a bit of research, effort, and planning, the following are steps sales professionals take to create their (ICP),

Step 1 - pull out a **list** of top 20% of companies that give you business, you can separate the top 20% by the standard measure of defining top performers used in your industry, e.g., in the hospitality industry the action for calculation would be the number of room nights a company gives a particular hotel,

Step 2 - learn from your team members/ boss/operations precisely **why** your top 20% clients are working with you, (in short identify what is it that we offer them so well that they like doing business with us)

e.g., in hotels, we would know that a client would do business with us if we're close to their office, or our incisions were better than what other hotels could offer, or our brand positioning was powerful with their customers. Factors such as client relationship, the aftersales service, the product attributes also count, the idea here is to make a list of reasons why they do business with us.

Step 3 do a thorough study in the following areas to ascertain your ICP,

a) Check with your delivery/operations/ aftersales / service teams about how it deals with these companies

b) Check with the finance team regarding their payment habits and expectations of these top clients.

c) Find out if there is a marketing strategy devised to acquire these accounts.

d) Study their firm history such as company size, industry segment, employee count, or annual turnover,

e) Also inquire about buying habits,(e.g., some companies have an onboarding process which goes on for six months, and some companies do it in two days) study about key influencers, reasons for continuing to do business with us (what is our perceived benefit by the market), current company value add on, buying cycle, buying process, levels of decision-makers involved

Keeping the above points as a benchmark, create your IDEAL CLIENT PROFILE

In other words, **identify the attributes of your best customers and plan towards bringing in more of those to your kitty**, if your company has multiple product lines you would have various ICP,

Once you have your ICP clearly defined, you can run it on your current prospect list, if your current prospect list has any account matching 80% of your ICP attributes then you should entirely focus on those clients first.

Following is a sample template of ICP, which you can use to create your own.

	Name of the company			
Sr No	**Firmographic**		**Buying Process**	
1	Industry		How many decision makers (Name designation)	
2	Location			
3	Annual Rev		Factors influencing buying decsion	
4	Employees			
5	Branches		Buying cycle	

	Customer pain point	Customer goal	How your solutions can help?
Point 1	[Example: They have a trouble managing the volume of transaction.]	[Example: They want to manage the volume in an efficient way to so that they can have optimum utilization of manpower for another task .]	[Example: We provide technology that does all the transaction with very less manual intervention, save time , money
Point 2			

ICP ANALYSIS TABLE

To analyze the potential of your current prospect list, you can judge them on the following parameters: this will help you if you have to disregard the client, develop them, or focus on them.

Disregard Develop Distinct

	Disregard	Develop	Distinct
Buyer Need	He is satisfied with his current set up	Has a pain area but does not hurt so mu	He has a business challenge that needs attention now
Buying cycle	Late buying decision	Solving his pain is not a priority for him	Deployment, the earlier the better
Budget	Has a poor Budget	Can afford	Can afford, can stretch as well

Buyer Need He is satisfied with his current set up Has a pain area but does not hurt so much He has a business challenge that needs attention now

Buying cycle Late buying decision-Solving his pain is not a priority for him Deployment, the earlier, the better

Buyer has an inadequate Budget Can afford can stretch as well.

For example, if you are calling a client and you know that they have a challenge but are not pressing them so much that they feel the need to change.

Also, if solving the problem is not a priority for them, but they have the potential to pay for your services. Your strategy for this account will be first to help them identify the pain (business problem), then make them realize if they don't solve it now, implications can get worse.

All clients in a distinct category should be on your top priority to close and do business.

When the client falls in the following category

Disregard – do not spend time on them, move them out of your focus list.

Develop – this will take a longer buying cycle, help them identify their pain, build on it, create urgency, make some effort, and follow up to move them to the distinct category,

Distinct - They are the ones you need to focus on entirely and have a prospecting plan.

If you are creating a new prospect list, you can prospect that is a close match to your ideal client profile sheet; this will give you better results.

Once you have a clear idea of who you want to reach out to, it's time we plan our next critical step, that is, prospecting,

> *"42% of sales pros say prospecting is the hardest part of their job. The rest say it's closing (36%) or qualifying (22%) (Hubspot)"*

Lets detail prospecting in our next section.

PROSPECTING

In geological terms, exploration is the first stage of getting essential minerals such as gold; in this phase, geologists analyze a predetermined territory to identify the presence of gold. The prospects then search for these minerals in this area, and once the expected fossil gets discovered, they sit by the water and search through mounds of dirt to find a few specks of gold.

Similarly, **sales prospecting is about identifying your gold (those who fit the ideal client profile) in a pre-defined territory.**

"42% of sales pros say prospecting is the hardest part of their job. The rest say it's closing (36%) or qualifying (22%) (Hubspot)",

Why most salespeople find it hard to prospect

1) **Irregular** - Average salespeople slack off the first two months of a quarter, then scramble in month three. Their third-month efforts get a lower success rate. (Gong)

2) **It is hard work** – On average, it takes 18 calls to reach a buyer. (TopoHQ), most of the amateur salespeople give up on the 4th try

3) **Scattered Hunting** – Remember that 50% of your prospects are not your right fit, amateur salespeople do not narrow down their search to match their ideal client profile. It triples the effort and reduces the probability of success

4) **Selling early** – The goal of a prospecting call is to build curiosity and set an appointment, that's it, amateur salespeople get into the flow on the first call itself, and 70% of the season buyers will talk price and demo on the first call itself, (selling or sharing amount without uncovering the buyer's needs is as good as the death of your sale)

5) **Connecting Right** – within and organization of up to 500 people, there is an average of 7 people responsible for buying decisions responsible for specific buying roles within the buying cycle. However, amateur salespeople focus on only one buyer,

Benefits Of Prospecting

Your sales pipeline is your sales lifeline. It is also interesting to note that, for various reasons, **a salesperson loses up to 20% of his regular business/clients every year (the leaking funnel concept).** Therefore, it becomes essential for a salesperson to keep a healthy pipeline for a constant flow of business.

Tools Of Prospecting – Some Interesting Statistics

Choosing the right tools for prospecting is essential; here are some interesting statistics on the usage of these tools by the sellers and buyers.

1) **Phone call** - A research by salesforce stated that 92% of all customer interactions happen over the phone, it is also the top 3 most preferred methods of connecting with clients, cold calling remains a widely used tool to communicate with your prospects, though it **takes an average of 8 cold calls to reach a prospect** (Baylor University)

2) **Email** – On an average, only about 25% of the clients open promotional sales email.

The effectiveness of an email lies in its customization, also remember the longer your email, the lesser chance of it getting read, the sweet spot is to have an email with a length of 50 – 125 words, also, if you want to get more responses, ask up to 3 questions in your email;

70 % of salespeople stop at one email. Yet if you send more emails, you've got a 25% chance to hear back. (YesWare)

3) **Social Media** – Here are some interesting facts on the usage of social media by the salespeople today

• More than 70% of sales pros use social selling tools like Facebook, Twitter, and LinkedIn. (State of Sales, LinkedIn)

• 72% of salespeople who use social media in their sales process outperform their peers.

• 50% of sales pros spend 3–10 hours per week using social selling tools. (State of Sales, LinkedIn)

• 84% of C-Level execs and 75% of B2B buyers use social media to make purchasing decisions. (Social Buying Meets Social Selling)

• The average B2B buyer who relies on social media to make buying decisions is senior, has a big budget, makes frequent purchases, and has more power to make buying decisions. (Social Buying Meets Social Selling)

4) **Data Banks** - such as fund data, and the most popular and highly used is your in house CRM; an adequately integrated and effectively utilized CRM can give you high yields in prospecting and building sales,

5) **Referral** - 84% of buyers now kick off their buying process with a reference.

After a positive experience, 83% of customers would be happy to provide a referral; sales champions realize the power of references, making sure they gather maximum referrals they can.

6) **Meet where your customer meets** - Know where your buyers are spending time, and become a part of their social gather-

ings/trade. Different committees such as (example only) MCCI, Indo German chambers of commerce, BNI, HR, Admin, Secretary groups, organize these gatherings on a periodical basis.

You are ready to prepare your prospecting guide, keeping in mind the **GASPS** formula and choosing your tools to **shortlist and connect with the client**

ASPS formula for prospecting

1) <u>Common **G**round</u> – they work towards finding common ground between them and the prospects, today with social media, it becomes, even more, practical to find a common interest and build a connect; eventually, sales is a peoples business, and people buy from people they like, when you join on common ground with people you build likeability

2) <u>**A**ppreciate routine</u> – successful salespeople make it a habit to prospect daily without fail, unless their sales pipeline is full to service existing clients, they set aside a block of time every day and cut themselves off from everything to focus on the calling – say, e.g., 8 am to 10 pm, etc.,

3) <u>Use a **S**cript</u> – making a script is the key to successful prospecting, it gives you mental preparedness to speak to the buyer in a concentrated flow, we will explore this point further in the upcoming chapter.

4) <u>**P**osition well</u> – Early in the call, they use tools to demonstrate themselves as valuable experts and provide compelling reasons for setting up their initial meetings.

Buyers do research online; still, they like to listen to capabilities that a product can solve and get insights from salespeople on their problems.

5) <u>Don't **Sell**</u> - They do not sell on the first call. Instead, they spend time in demonstrating that they have an attitude of service and are available to listen to the buyer's problems

Once you have done identifying your client get ready with a killer introduction machine, your elevator pitch in the upcoming chapter

ELEVATOR PITCH

Your elevator pitch is a 30-second memorable description of what you do and what you sell.

Objective of this description is to **earn a second conversation**, with the client,

What is the origin of this "sales story" – once a sales rep was going on a sales call to a large Fortune 500 company, He gets into an elevator and guess who steps in next to him? The CEO of that company!!

It was the best opportunity for him to introduce himself and his company offerings, but he had not more than 40 seconds before the elevator hits the top floor. What does he tell the CEO? Hence the elevator pitch concept was born.

It states that you must be able to articulate to someone what you do and provide value in one minute or less. I argue that the best people have a good 30 and 60-second pitch.

You have got to continually be selling your product, without making people feel too uncomfortable.

You can meet your prospect anywhere, over a phone call, at a social gathering, in the marketplace or a bar, you should be able to make the right impact in the first go itself.

The elevator pitch is a potent tool used for personal branding, company introduction, and business introduction.

Let us go through a step by step guide help you prepare yours,

Before we start let us see some important points about the elevator pitch

1) Do not try to close a deal

2) It's about the client and not you – do not try to brag about your self or your company in an elevator pitch, instead just focus on the what value you bring to clients, we will speak more on that in the upcoming pages

3) The longer your pitch, the lesser chance you can strike a meaningful conversation, 30 – 45 seconds is ideal.

Keeping these things in mind, now let's work on the elements of a good elevator pitch.

1) While introducing **keep information about yourself minimum,** E.g., I represent XYZ Firm, {and a maximum 10-word description about your company}, "we are a corporate hospitality solution provider."

2) **Your customer** – You need to focus on who your target customer is and what problems they face. For, e.g., my customers are corporate MNC, and common challenges my customer faces is buying travel services at the right price.

Therefore, my elevator pitch would be something like – I represent XYZ Travel, a corporate hospitality solution provider, we help MNC save up to 10% on their overall hospitality spending annually.

3) **Solve problem** – you need to mention to the client what makes your business unique? And how you solve the problem you have mentioned above, always put numbers if you can.

4) **You can specify your key USP,** e.g., we can say that "we optimize cost by leveraging bulk buying and distribution of hotel rooms and ground transportation services and pass on the cost

benefits to our clients.

5) **Have a hook** – towards the end of the pitch, ask an engaging question, or make them ask you a question that brings them to think about your offering.

e.g., Mr. client do you know outsourcing of services can bring in operational efficiency and save cost at the same time; we are the leaders in corporate hospitality solutions. We have been able to help more than 500 MNC in the country to save high cost.

Alternatively, you can also tell them something unusual: that builds curiosity, so that they ask you how, what, and why question after your statement.

E.g., Mr client, you know we have been able to save all bring in process efficiency in hospitality bookings for all my clients?

6) **Call to action** – Build an opportunity to follow up, an elevator pitch helps to introduce yourself in an impactful way and schedule the next meeting, so to ask for an action, you may request for a question like

• Maybe we should evaluate your booking process together. What's your availability next week?"

• "Since you're interested, let me come over to your office and discuss more in detail; what's the next best slot available on your calendar?"

Here are a buyer and a seller who casually caught up at an exhibition, after exchanging greetings the conversation goes as

• Customer: "Hey, Rakesh. Good to see you, what brings you to this procurement seminar?"

• Seller: "We're here because many MNC;s use our system to reduce their travel cost 10%. We buy and sell on bulk, so corporates stand to get a lot of rate advantages working with us

• Customer: "Hmm... that's interesting by travel do you mean airlines."

• Seller: "Ya airlines, and much more, its hotels, cars, and event management to be precise ?"

• Customer – Sounds interesting, have you got a chance to visit Vikas from the office he takes care of all this, I am sure he could use some of your services

• Seller – Sure, I haven't met him yet, can you connect me to him, I will write to you, and we can then take it forward from there

• Customer – done deal, do send me an email I will path you guys up

Elevator pitch is a handy tool for personal branding. It helps you introduce yourself on a networking platform in a very impactful way. Here are two examples of a personal introduction: one introduction without an elevator pitch and the other one with the help of an elevator pitch,

choose which one will be more effective for you.

Option 1

Acquaintance - Hey so what do you do

I am a sales head with a leading hospitality brand, managing a team that delivers high service and revenue growth of 10% every year.

Acquaintance - That sounds awesome Rakesh, (By this sentence what the client means is that it's the hundredth time today I hear someone bragging about being an X with Y years of experience in Z firm.),

They are bored to death; as you see, this introduction has not left any impact on them, so the conversation runs dry.

Or here is another option for the same conversation

Option 2

Acquaintance – hey, what do you do?

Me – Do you know that with best systems and process in place there is a 2.7% escalation rate in the ground travel business

Acquaintance – Oh I see!

Me – to bridge the gap we have implemented systems to have 99% accuracy rate, I represent sales for ABC travel company that has help over 300 MNC's to better manage the ground handling and save cost up to 10%.

Acquaintance – oh great, we have been looking to curtail costs in travel, it will be worthwhile to take some suggestion.

Me – sure let me know your calendar this Friday, will be happy to discuss this at your office,

Acquaintance – sure (and the conversation continues)

Here's how to make a personal elevator pitch:

1. Start your elevator pitch with something that grabs attention and builds rapport, like a common problem in your industry everyone, will be familiar.

2. Spark curiosity by saying that you solve this problem.

3. Say who you are and what you do.

4. Explain how you do it and what the results are.

5. Be ready to answer questions: you need to keep the conversation going.

6. Always have a business card at hand.

Use the PAR (Problem—Action—Result) formula. First, introduce the widely relevant problem, then show actions you have taken to solve the problem, and then speak about the results generated by your activities, this helps make it more conversational.

Every pitch needs practice to become competent, so don't get upset if you are not getting what you want on the first go, you can change and edit your script as many times you deem fit, The more you practice it, the more naturally it will flow from you,

SETTING APPOINTMENTS

Appointment setting is challenging for most salespeople. Getting this wrong can delay your entire sale cycle with a prospect. Also, it's your first interaction with the client, so getting this part right is vital for setting the tone of your sale. Mostly, "presentation of your product is a lesser challenge than getting to the presentation."

Let us look at the top 4 reasons for a buyer not to give us an appointment.

1)**Mental Defense** - Prospects feel that the person calling to set up a meeting is trying to take away something from me (usually money, or will force me to buy something I don't want, etc.)

Solution – an ideal approach by the seller be of building rapport and establishing the trust that where the client realizes that you want to help him not cheat

2)**Poor First Impression** - You create your first impression in the first few seconds of your call, your tone, confidence, and attitude matter while making appointments.

A person with a low energy, less enthusiasm, non-planned script, and a fearful /hesitant tone is likely to get a higher decline rate

Solution – prepare your text before calling

3)**They are too busy**- most buyers get multiple calls daily and buying your product is never their first plan,

Solution - The key to overcoming this barrier is to acknowledge that their time is essential and that you are trying to turn this interruption into a scheduled conversation at their earliest convenience.

Tell them, "I know you're busy." Acknowledge that you are an interruption. Be quick and brief in your elevator pitch.

Respect their time, and they will respect you. If your clients ask you to call back, make sure you do take their phone number and email id for a callback.

4)**You get connected to the wrong person** – This happens if your research is not intense. You get connected to the non-decision maker or a person who is not involved in the direct buying process. In such a scenario, ask for the person in charge

Solution – In case you do not know the correct decision-maker, you can ask the person on the phone, here is an example

Sam – I am sorry I don't look into these elements

Me- I am sorry to bother you, but can you tell me who would make the right decision on this topic,

Sam – It would be Mr. Raj from the marketing department,

Me – Can you give me his number? I am sure I have a new solution for him.

Sam – Not sure if I can give you his number, but you can just drop him an email on abc@xxxx.com

Me – thanks can I give him your reference

Sam – Sure go-ahead

Me – thanks, it was nice talking to you.

Remember that setting appointments is simple – but not easy; you need to be patient with your buyers and keep trying.

Practical tips on appointment setting

1) **Start by asking** -,, "I understand you're in charge of [their title of responsibility like sales or marketing], is that right?" Asking about their designation does two things: first, it confirms you are speaking to the right person and second strokes their ego, usually the answer would be a yes and psychologically he would be interested in listening to your next point

2) **Bring in your Elevator Pitch** – it is your 30-second introduction speech that you can use on your client to get your first impression correct and generate curiosity. Please refer to the elevator pitch section for a detailed information

3) **80/20 rule works just well**, - whenever on a call with your prospect, a good salesperson will do the 20% of talking and 80% of listening, moreover they will make the prospect feel they have heard them by paraphrasing their requests.

4) **Always have a valid reason for an appointment** – I have listened to many salespeople taking appointments like,

Hi Ms. Kumar, how are you? I am Ajay from ABD transport solutions; I wanted to make your appointment and meet you today?

in actuality, your client hears you as (Hi Ms. Kumar, I don't have a plan today, I have a lot of off-budget pressure, I want to desperately run out of my office to see if you can give me some business)

Have a plan that (shouts out loud to the client what is in it for them) to have this meeting

Always find a benefit for the listener, address your call keeping in mind the problem they would be facing and tell them that you could have probable solutions for these problems,

E.g., Hi am I speaking with Ms. Kumar, heading travel services for Cybage India

Mrs. Kumar – Yes, may I know who is talking,

Me – Hi, this is Rakesh from Skill transport solutions. We provide transport solutions to various companies in India. We realize that we could save you cost and bring efficiency to your transport process. Can I come over and discuss in detail about this on this week?

Also, when you want a meeting, ask for it; **don't let the client assume that you wish for the meeting,** e.g., considering the above example if I would have ended the conversation with so Mrs.Kumar so what do you think ?, instead of asking (can I come over)

I am sure the conversation would have mostly ended as why don't you send me an email on this,

Be specific to ask, can we meet (on the day) and (time) to discuss this in-depth.

5) **Scarcity sells** – always create scarcity while giving options to the client, like we have a limited period offer and I wanted you to have the best advantage of it,

Or in case they are asking you to call back Give them two options only – whenever a client tell you to reschedule your appointment give them options on your calendar

You - "Great. Sachin, I know you're busy right now how is your schedule placed next Monday for 10-15 minutes for a quick call.

Client – Monday looks fine

You – would you prefer the first half or second half,

Client – 2 pm is good

You – Noted, thanks have a great evening.

6) **Call back when needed** – Have a reliable follow-up mechanism, never miss to call back when the client has asked you to call later,

"80% of the deals require five follow-up calls after a meeting. 44% of salespeople give up after one follow up" (Source: The

Marketing Donut)

Prospects are busier than ever, thanks to technology. They are loaded with marketing information and meeting vendors. Therefore, it's unlikely you break through the noise, but it's unlikely you will do so on your first try.

Several appointment setters like to close by asking closed questions like: Will it be possible to meet so we can discuss your business more? This question calls for a yes or no answer.

Instead, try asking something like: Which day would be best for you, Thursday or Friday? Without realizing it, most of them will give you their preferred date and time.

7) **Meeting Invite** – Always send a meeting invite over an email once the prospect confirms the rally.

8) **Call Timing Matters** - Reach out during "off hours": Business leaders don't punch in at nine and out at five. The gatekeepers, however, are a different story. If you're trying to get through to a busy executive, try calling early in the morning (before 9 am), late in the evening (after 7 pm), or during lunch, there is a higher chance of being connected.

Never Stop Learning; everyone develops their strategy of taking appointments. Only constant practice can tell you what works for you and what you can change.

There is no correct way to do this. The point is to have a keen eye for detail. If you make a mistake, take note and don't repeat it. If you find something that works, keep doing it, and while you are at it, see better and more natural ways of doing it. Here are a few noteworthy examples:

PREPARATION

"By failing to prepare, you are preparing to fail." - Benjamin Franklin

Many salespeople skip this process; they jump right from taking an appointment to meeting the prospect without preparation.

Not preparing for a meeting has multiple risks involved; among the other factors, the most significant threat we run is of providing a generalized solution to the prospect which doesn't differentiate us from our competitors.

"Nearly 57% of B2B prospects and customers feel that their sales teams are not prepared for the first meeting." (Source: IDC)

Let us see how the buyer perceives us when we do not prepare for the call,

1) When the offering is not customized the buyer will not feel connected many may feel the need to look out at more options, the seller loses his chance to move up the buying process, and instead of eradicating competition the seller himself becomes a reason to invite competition for him indirectly

2) Buyer immediately categorizes the seller as a "generalist" because the seller has not been able to establish positioning correctly in the meeting,

3) The buyer may perceive the seller to be non-confident or non-interested in his product or offerings

4) Buyers may view the seller to be non-trustworthy

Benefits of preparation for the meeting /presentation

1) **First impressions are lasting impressions** – your sale moves faster if you can demonstrate to the buyer that you are genuinely interested in solving their problem. That only happens once you are well prepared to uncover his problems

2) **Builds trust** – being ready for the call puts you in a better position to identify the client's pain areas; listening and understanding the buyer gives him confidence and builds credibility and trustworthiness

"The average sales conversion rate across all industries is 2.46%–3.26% (Statista)," i.e., every 100 accounts you prospect, you will close about 3.

With a closure rate of only 3%, you can judge how important it is to prepare before the call.

Some handy tips to prepare for your call,

A real worth of a sales meeting would be when the client would pay for a meeting with you,

to have a compelling sales call, you need to keep the following things in mind

1) **Know your meeting objective** – Most importantly know what you want to derive from the meeting for yourself,

you need to ask if this a need/discovery meeting, or is this a relationship-building call, or a rate neg meeting, or a new business meeting, etc.

Every meeting should be able to take the sale forward for a closure, or else it may not be a productive meeting.

Before stepping into the meeting, you should,

Know what you want to derive as an outcome from this meeting and plan yourself accordingly,

Know the time the meeting should take and the flow of question

Know the information required to set the tone of the meeting,

Be well prepared with your marketing collateral and supporting documents.

If you do not know what outcome you desire from this meeting, then please don't go for the meeting.

2) **Know what your prospect wants** – You should be able to set the list with the client and know what is he expecting out of this meeting, plan preferably should be drafted and sent on an email before the meeting, If need be you may also want to send in your presentation that you are going to deliver before the meeting,

3) **Prepare for a desired outcome** - Depending on your meeting objective and your desired outcome, BE MENTALLY PREPARED HOW YOU WOULD WANT THE MEETING TO GO, Successful salespeople complete the session in their head before actually going for the meeting

If it's a rate neg, - have you planned for the like price, have you mapped for your free add ons that you want to give away, have you scheduled for reiteration of the most significant pain you are solving for them.

If it's a rapport building call – have you picked up a souvenir for the client, have you done a profile search on their likes and dislikes, have you learned about a common ground of interest for both.

4) Meeting the right connect

At the end of every meeting, a salesperson would like a commitment in line with his objectives. Therefore, it is essential to meet the right person in the correct position to provide necessary input.

For example, if you need general factual information about the company (such as current systems, vendors, set up, etc.), are you meeting the lower line guy who is in the capacity, interest, and time to provide necessary information to you.

On the other hand, a decision-maker will not be interested or available to give you such knowledge, so it is critical to determine the person you are taking an appointment, which is in the capacity to fulfill your objective.

What to Do After a Meeting

How would you judge if your meeting has gone well?

A general indicator of a good meeting is that if a client has agreed to a next action step that progress your sales to a closure, the meeting has been successful.

And yes, while it is essential to have a scheduled next level, you must also evaluate your performance.

Here is a guideline checklist to ask yourself after the call.

• Did I meet with the right decision-maker(s) or "product approvers?"

• Did I uncover information about:

o Are they buying criteria?

o Buying process.

o Budget?

o Timetable for decision?

Ask yourself if you saw any non-verbal buying signals, you should also assess and score the prospect's viability to move the deal forward. E.g., I was in a big deal last year had a massive turnover for our company, it took us three months to come to a closure only to realize that we will not be able to go through the detail,

The reason was that as per an onboarding policy client needed a minimum of 6months to get a vendor onboarded, and the event was next month.

Therefore, we always need to ask the right questions, listen for understanding, build credibility, and advance the opportunity through creating a scheduled next step.

DISCOVERY CALL

If sales is a process of disqualification of leads, discovery meeting is the qualification point, these calls set the direction for your sales,

The principal objective of this call is to

• Identify buyers pain points in-depth,

• Learn about their business goals

• Most importantly, demonstrate that you could have a probable solution for their problems.

It is not mandatory to do the discovery calls, but these calls become important if

• There are multiple decision-makers

• You have more competitors

• When the money spend is moderate to high, and they have a small decision-making time frame.

Importance of a discovery call.

I have seen many salespeople entirely skipping this step, and assuming problems, priorities and goals the clients would have,

Without understanding these areas, they cannot customize presentations for the client, and risk the opportunity to set their positioning against their competitor.

If done well, this gives control of the sales process to the seller; however, if not done well, you are at the mercy of the buyer.

Decoding the discovery call,

While this call has its importance in the sales cycle, execution of this call would be a little different from presentation meetings or rate negotiation meeting, etc.,

This call is about asking the right question to get the most appropriate responses to your customers' current situation,

Let us decode the elements of successful discovery call,

1)Focused research

Demerit of not doing research is that the seller will spend a lot of his calling time uncovering the necessary information, which the seller could have quickly taken from multiple other sources,

Many amateur salespeople spend maximum time discovering these questions: How many employees you have, where are your offices in the country, what products you are into, what the turnover is, who is the primary decision-maker, etc.

This information can be provided to you by the company marketing collateral/website. You can also speak to the junior staff who would be more available and interested in sharing such information with you.

While you are studying the company on the internet make sure you also run though buyers LinkedIn profile and google search on them, this will give you a lot of common connect points or talking points at the start of the meeting.

2)Appreciate – Check - End

For the customer to give you maximum information you need to make them feel that they would be in control of the call, you need to express this point very clearly right from the time start of the meeting; clients get reserved in sharing information when they feel the salesperson is trying to sell them products they don't need

I have seen some salespeople conducting a discovery call as an interrogation routine; the client needs to open up and trust you to share information; therefore it becomes essential to set the tone right from the introduction itself

Your opening sentence should take about 45 seconds — here's a great framework to get started inspired by Hiro Rodriguez.

ACE: Call Opening

A - **Appreciate** you taking the time for today's call.

C- **Check End Time** "We have 15 minutes scheduled to speak today — does that work for you?

E - **End Goal** - "The end goal of this meeting is to understand your requirements to see how we can potentially help.

3) 45 – 55 rule of Discovery

"Discovery is about asking 45% and listening 55%."

Before uncovering root problems, your conversation flow usually goes into revealing three layers; now that you have researched to discover their current situation, let's take a deep dive into the other layers.

• **Qualification Layer** – it is about knowing their current business status. Therefore your questions will revolve around knowing their ongoing process, people involved in managing those processes and time and money spent while in the process, you should spend less than 10 - 15% of your time on this section.

Some, e.g., are as follows,

➢ How do you manage your current spends,

➢ Do you have systems in place

➢ Can you throw some light on significant task done day by your team daily

➢ How many people are involved in managing these bookings

➢ What is round cost you allocate to these activates

• **Challenge / Problem Layer** – Once you understand their process you need to know why are they looking for a change or highlight to them why should they be looking for a change, your correct analysis of the client situation will determine your positioning you can build with your client, if they feel that there is not a problem with their process, you can also lead them to potential future issues that can develop if they don't choose to act on it now, you can spend about 50 – 60 % of your call on this section, Some examples of these question would be

➢ Don't you think if you use a little technical support, you could be saving a lot of your time

➢ Tell me honestly how much time this work consumes, does it impact your other work delivery schedules

➢ Is controlling cost a part of your KRA, how do you think you will be able to achieve that with this current set up you have

These questions will start to open possible problem areas of the client, you can expose that pain points and will be the foundation for your following presentation

Also, remember that the successful sales managers uncovered three to 3 – 4 problems per client, which directly correlates with the sale's success. Sales superstars do not stop at this layer, and they go onto uncovering one more final layer of pain.

• **Benefit Layer** - This phase counts because it has a direct correlation between your offering and their need, its, making them accept that they don't have what you have got to offer. If done right you know you will be in command of the sale all through till the end, you should spend about 20 – 30% of your time on this section, an excellent way to uncover this is by asking them what-if questions?

➤ For Eg, they have agreed that their most significant pain area is wastage of time in managing bookings and you know at the back of your head that your product is supported by technology that does 80% of the job they are doing manually indirectly saving their time, so your question can be

➤ What if you had a process where you did not have to make the bookings manually, how would that help you?

These questions direct clients to speak about the benefit of your product without knowing what you have to offer.

Smart sales manager asks up to 3 questions that highlight what the client would miss out on if they did not buy your product.

For Eg, you know that the befit of using your product is price plus service, and you can ask questions like

What if you saved about 7 – 8 % on your monthly spending? How would that impact your teams KRA. What if you saved about 150 mins on doing calculations every day, how would that help your organization?

4) Share an Experience

When it comes to sharing information on Layer 2 or Layer 3, some clients may not open up entirely due to several factors, Sales superstars use this opportunity to share an experience about how they were able to help another client of a similar industry, but during this experience, they focus more on the problems faced by the other clients and less on the solutions they offer, because discovery call is about the client, the more they speak, the better it is for our success

Experience sharing is more like a route rectifier. It helps if the call is not going in the desired direction or bail a salesperson out if he ever gets in a tongue-tied situation.

For E.g.

"We've just been working with Zen Soft company since the past six months as too many of their travelers were not satisfied with their existing car service provider, and they assumed that the vendor was not capturing many of their bookings information in the right manner, this led to delayed services furious internal employees, duplication of bills, etc.,

How do you manage the entire transport piece at your organization.?"

5. ASK

The real value of a discovery call would be when you are invited for a presentation to discuss potential solutions that you may have for the client, also advance this call to a sale,

It always ideal for summarizing specific areas in which you feel your product or service will be of value and then ask for the next meeting,

I have seen amateur salespeople completing the call and not asking for the next meeting.

In contrast, the entire idea of doing a discovery call is to advance the sales discussion to the presentation stage. We get a face to face opportunity with their decision-makers to convince them for a close.

Here are a few examples of the asking the client at the end of the call

Summarize the problem, highlight the implication, demonstrate that you can fix it, ask for a meeting,

"Ms. Jyoti, based on our discussion today about your long booking process and scattered buying of hotel rooms, how you feel this needs to be more streamlined to curtail cost and have better technology to manage the manual work.

I think this is an area we can impact massively; can we schedule this week with you and your team of decision-makers so I can show you how our solutions can affect your goals positively.

"Mr. Mehta – you mentioned that you simply don't have the time to sit in on the compile the MIS of your transactions, yet you feel this critical step to control cost better and make your teams more accountable.

If I could demonstrate how we have helped other companies address this exact problem, is that something you would want to see?"

Please do make sure that you request them to invite other stakeholders for this meeting too, and it will also be handy to learn more about these stakeholders from your point of contact before the next meeting.

Once we have identified our clients' challenges and know how to solve them, let's get ready for our next big meeting which is Presentation stage,

FOLLOW UP

Does this happen to you? We think that we have done an excellent job by sending out an email to that outstanding prospect, or by doing the first presentation with our client, or by making that call for a meeting, now it's time to feel good and wait for them to respond.

If the client does not respond and is an important one, we may send him a casual email/text or a call hoping to hear a positive response.

If, after about one or two follow-ups, we still do not hear from him, assuming that he is not interested in our offerings, we move on to the next one.

It is interesting to note that as per a survey 92% of the clients do not respond in the first five attempts

Here is the exact break up according to Marketing Donut

• 44% of sales reps stop following up after one rejection or ignored email

• 22% of reps stop after two attempts

• 14% of reps stop after three attempts

• 12% of reps stop after four attempts

Yes, you got that right, only 8% of the salespeople are getting

80% of the business, because they follow-up

But somewhere we know this, don't we? But what is more surprising it that salespeople still do not follow up **assertively**, here are some reasons I could identify

• If they do not have a proper follow-up system in place, they **FORGET to follow up.**

• **Fear of losing the client or rejection** - Eventually, it comes to the thought of what if my follow-ups annoy the client or if he thinks I am not giving him a decision-making space?

He may never buy from me if I come across as too pushy. It may even put my relationship with him in an uncomfortable situation.

I understand these thoughts, **but we need to know that all these beliefs are just assumptions until we do not hear a direct response from the client.**

As a salesperson, we always need to remember that by following up, we are helping our clients make a business decision, and it is entirely okay to follow up. It's our job to maintain the relationship and move the conversation forward.

That is how you get things done that others don't. That's how you get meetings that others don't. You follow up. And you never stop until you get the job done!

I am putting this section as a compilation of some important questions asked about Following up with the client. Please note QNA is not hard and fast rules but general guidelines, which, if followed well, can get you better sales success.

Question - Till when should you follow up?

Answer - I suggest that if it's a cold call, three times by email and three times by phone/text, beyond that, I don't think we have earned the right to follow up with the client.

But if I have a relationship with the client, I will follow up until I get a response, and I believe that if they have a reason not to buy, they also have time to share that reason with me. If a client tells me he will let me know in 10 days, I will mark it on my calendar and follow up on the 11th day,

I am not saying that I want to be pushy or get stuck on people until they buy,

I am entirely against pressuring them into a purchase, but I am trying to say that **I do not want to assume that the client does not want to buy from me unless he tells me himself,**

Do not contact me; I am not interested in the product, I cannot make a purchasing decision right now, are all acceptable answers to end my follow up chase with the client,

Question - What is the best method of follow up?

Answer – It depends on the outcome you are looking at, if you have done your initial meeting and are looking at an urgent response, then a phone call is the best option. But keep in mind that phone calls put more pressure on the buyer, repetitive usage can also put them off even if they were interested in buying from you in the first place, so my advice is to use it only when you are looking at an urgent response.

A little lesser pressuring method will be to follow up on a text message or a WhatsApp; the client gets their time to respond. Also, like phone calls even here, there is a thin line between being perceived as assertive or pushy, so use text messages thoughtfully. It is easier to manage phone calls and text when you have established a relationship with the buyer.

I am not a big fan of following up through social media, we are all humans, and personal life needs to be distinct from professional follow-ups. I may only want to use LinkedIn sparingly to connect but never to follow up.

I see a few salespeople landing uninvited in their client's office on the pretext of a follow-up for a potential buyer's response. Yes, I believe that face to face conversation is the most impactful; however, you also run the risk of being perceived as desperate or needy for a response, so use this step only if extremely necessary.

Emails are one of the most used follow-up methods, here are some ways to write useful follow-up emails

1) **Subject Line** – keep it short of up to 3 words, keep it relevant to the email's objective.

2) **Email Body** – Keep it short, upbeat, and professional, buyers don't read long emails, 75 - 100 words are good enough (again just a guideline, not a rule), the focus should be to speak on the point quickly.

3) **Don't just ask, "Share"** – when a buyer reads a line such as, Hi Raj, just wanted to check if you got a chance to review your proposal, look forward to hearing your response at the earliest, it does not generate desire for him to act on your email

Instead, if he gets to see things like, hi Raj, here sharing with you a one-minute video of how our products have befitted clients in your industry? I will be happy to know If these could benefit you as well.

I will be happy to know about your experience.

Point I am trying to make is instead of just asking, first, give

Make sure you complete the email/call/text with an action request, e.g.; please do share an update proposal sent or, can you set up a meeting with the senior management for further discussion.

4) **Break – Up email** – after three attempts, you need to let the prospect know that you have tried getting in touch with them, but since we could not hear from, we understand their priorities and would not bother them, as this may not be the best time to connect.

It like telling them this is the last time we are trying to connect with you; many times, this email may get you the maximum response.

But the thought behind this email is to let them know that we respect their space while keeping an open door for future business.

Multiple connect – it's recommended to reach out to numerous touchpoints in a company, which increases your probability of getting a response and closure. During your ideal client profiling phase, once you have identified all the buyers in your target company, please feel free to write to all of them.

Here are some general Do's and Don'ts of follow-ups

Do's

1) **Do respect your clients time** – give your buyer a reasonable time frame to respond, do not spam their email, like a good thumb rule should be about 48 hours per email.

2) **Do stay professional** – have an approach of indifference to non-responses.

3) **Do ensure your content is relative** – please ensure that follow-up emails focus on the client's needs and always aim to deliver value in every transaction.

4) **Create a system that reminds you about follow**-ups on a timely basis and makes optimum use of your smartphones and CRMs to create a reliable follow-up system.

5) Most importantly, do always remain in a state of persistence and positivity .

Do Not

1) **Do not – send long emails,** constant messages, copy-paste emails; clients find these meaningless and non-valuable

2) **Do not make them feel guilty** – of not responding to you, do

not mention phrases like, I have been trying to reach you since ten days but no response, can you let me know if you have an update for me on this? Etc.

PRESENTATION

In a recent project at my current organization, I had volunteered to visit the neighboring market and observe new salespeople on the field, which gave me and them an opportunity to learn more about the selling process and help each other.

I want to share with you an interesting conversation with you about my first sales call there,

It was a two-day visit. I reached office at 855 am on day one as I had pre-scheduled sales calls with Sr Sales resource of my company,

15 min later when our Sr Sales resource comes in we directly jump on to discussing the call plan for the day, during our discussion I learned that our first call is at a 45 min drive time away and it a presentation on an upcoming event, this meeting is with a group of people including Head HR, Marketing head along with Travel services head and one member from their team each,

Presentation meetings are my favorite because, in these meetings, a salesperson can own the discussion and steer it to his desired outcome.

While it was 9:30 already and our first meeting was scheduled at 10:30 am, I insisted that we get going on our way,

We sort of caught up on the meeting agenda while driving in the car, I was the shotgun, my colleague was driving, here is a snippet of the conversation.

Me – who all do you know are also pitching in for this event.

Salesperson – Not sure actually, we can find out today, honestly, I have just had a brief round of discovery call with them last week, could not judge much,

Me – No worries, what is the event about

Salesperson – It's an annual event where they invite families and conduct RNR for their top performers!!

Me- Great, I am sure they would have a reasonable budget, would you know who did this event form them last year, where did it happen (location) and how many people attended (these details can give us an idea on the spend capacity of the client)

Salesperson – Honestly, I only have got a brief for this year, I don't know if they even did an event last year

Me -I am sure they would have, it is an annual event, they may have done it last year too - just out of curiosity why do you think they want to try us?

Sales peon -I guess they did not have a great experience with their previous vendor partners; in my last meeting, I overheard the two talking about the food quality, which was a disappointment.

Me – Okay, do we have a presentation ready for this meeting?

Salesperson – oh, of course, I always carry our marketing deck, we will take them through our other events.

Me – oh, haven't we made a customized deck for them? (customization gives us the leverage for a presentation)

Salesperson – Our designer was caught up as this was a last-minute request raised by the company

While the conversation continued, we were in the buyers building at 10:20, looking for parking. While trying to enter the premises, we were immediately guided outside the gate, as all the parking slots in the building were full, so we had to look for a car park outside.

Me – Wouldn't it have been better to share our car details and arrival time with the company so that they could have had a slot reserved for us,

Salesperson – hey, that's a good idea. Sorry completely skipped out of my mind.

While the both of us walked in our tailored blue suits gathering our laptops and brisk walking our way through the building it was 1030 am already,

While we were getting frisked at the building entrance, the security had our details so we could enter, but they did not have our laptop details, so the colleague had to call up the client and give them our laptop details about 7 min of our time.

While on the way to the meeting rooms from the security I told my colleague, hey buddy, since you have met the client before and know about their requirements would you like to lead the presentation today and I will take a back seat and jump in where ever need,

Oh No problem he yelled with excitement, that will be a great experience,

By 10 42am, we reached the board room where about five panelists were sitting on one side of the table.

We sat on the other side of the table, after exchanging our greeting,

HR Head - Before the meeting starts, I want to let you guys know that I have a schedule at 11 am, I will move on buy my team can continue for the discussion

Salesperson No worries Mr. Sharma, we will get to the presentation right on, can you pass me the HDMI connector please said the salesperson.

Hr Head - We do not have an HDMI we do have a VGA will that

work, or should we call the IT to fix it asked the HR Head

Sales Peron - Sir I guess we need to call the IT because my laptop does not support the VGA output,

Well, by 10:53 am with all the setup, the meeting started.

My colleague took them through the entire slides of the presentation, and we concluded by 11 33 am, I was keeping the time as I didn't have much to do, I was just a silent spectator.

Almost about twice during the meeting pricing was discussed and we were occasionally compared with one or two competitors,

At the end of the meeting, the client said there are also evaluating a couple of other vendors would get back to with final shortlisting within two days.

After nodding our heads and exchanging greetings, we left from the meeting room,

After the meeting we went down to grab a cup of tea, my colleague in his highest excitement and a big smile asked me,

How did you like the presentation, Rakesh?

Me – if you want me to be honest, I don't think we will be winning the bid unless the other guys who are pitching to them are entirely new to their field or do not turn up for this meeting, I think there is a lot of scope of improvement in our presentation,

After I shared my feedback with him for the next 30 min, there was silence in the car till we reached another meeting, and also by the end my 2-day trip we learned that the client had given the bid to another vendor partner,

My colleague came to me and asked me what you think went wrong in our presentation; that is when I asked him to cheer up and took him through effective presentation methods mentioned in this chapter.

These techniques are a compilation of some best practices used by some successful sales super starts for making effective presentations.

Skilled salespeople master the art of presentation. I **call it art because every induvial can create their unique presentation by using the primary key ingredients of making an effective sales presentation**, and when done in the right manner creates a lot of sales success, closure and bring in more revenue.

These key ingredients of a successful sales presentation are – 4 C's

• A Compelling story

• Highlighting a Customized value proposition

• Suiting in line with the client's needs

• Ending in a call to action which leads to an advancement of a sales

Sales Presentation Techniques

1) **Set the context before you present** – Successful salespeople realize that the meeting is about setting credibility, bringing out logic through correct identification of the buyers' problem in the identification phase or the research that the seller has already done,

They always set the prelude right by taking care of the basics such as being available for the presentation 10 min before on time, ensuring they have ready everything necessary for the meeting including the right connectors for laptops, etc., making sure all the essential data required for presentation is already open before the meeting and have a customized presentation

salespeople should always introduce the reason for the meeting and ask the client what their critical expectations or expected outcomes are.

I have also seen some of them sending their presentations to the client beforehand contrary to the popular belief that the client will not be interested in the meeting once he reads the presentation

On the contrary, I have seen it work in favor of the salesperson often where they start with the introduction right from where the buyer wants it to be,

Solving questions and objections early in the meeting is more beneficial than raising objections

in the during the commitment stage.

2) **Plan your presentation** – the best way to plan a presentation meeting is by referencing the topics the buyers highlighted on the discovery call. Start with the most important one first and work your way through the lesser important ones.

Also during your discovery if you have identified 3 to 4 problems you need to start with the most important ones first to the client, once you can win their trust on the most critical topic the other topics get less resistance and are a smooth sail through,

Also please remember you are in charge of your presentation so you can choose to change the flow during the presentation as well,

3) **Follow AIDA**

AIDA is a very logically driven process to plan your presentation; all you need to do is follow the flow; it stands for Attention, Interest, Desire Action, here is what it means.

Attention – Grab their attention early in the meeting with a grand opening by focusing on the problem (which you learned about in your discovery call) and promise them the solution you have for them

Interest – to have an impact on the client you need to maintain their attention throughout to keep your presentation interesting you use the following steps

a) Communication about you should be relevant enough to build credibility, however, should not cover more than 10 % of your presentation,

b) things to avoid are your company achievements, flashy charts showing your progress, your company history, photographs showing your company building, etc.

c) Always remember this presentation is about YOUR CLIENT, so keep focusing on them in the entire presentation.

d) Sometimes, during presentations, salespeople tend to get into monologues, making the clients disinterested quickly, always keeping the conversation as a dialogue to ensure maximum interest is maintained, and keeping asking enrolling questions throughout the presentation,

e) With an ever-reducing attention span of humans, experts mention that in 2019 the average attention span dropped lasting about 7 minutes before you run the risk of losing them. You might keep them interested for 10 minutes if the topic is unusual, or just 5 minutes if you're presenting that sleepy post-lunch period, so always keep your presentation for a maximum of 10 min,

f) To keep their interest in the presentation, you can

• Get feedback in between

• Do not have a lot of data on the presentation slides; keep it more visual.

Desire – Before giving the solution, you always evoke curiosity for the buyer to know more; through compelling storytelling, which revolves around the client's problems and the benefit of your product.

After presenting the solution, you can immediately top it up with testimonials from other clients; this ensures that enough desire is built to generate curiosity and action for your products.

Action – the best sale is the sale that gets closed; the whole idea of the presentation is to solicit client engagement. I have seen many salespeople leaving the room without an appropriate request for a call to action. If they don't act, your entire presentation makes the buyer more educated about the product and gives him a chance to buy from the next seller who comes in.

3. Invoke Emotion

I used to see many salespeople focusing on the Features, Advantages, and Benefits. I used to see presentations with a lot of company information and slide after slide data. Often, the client would lose interest in the display during the first 10 minutes itself,

today in a digital age where the buyer already gets influenced on his buying decision 57% of the time before meeting a single salesperson, thanks to readily available information,

Therefore, it becomes more and more important to differentiate ourselves and have an emotional connection with the buyer

; this can happen with compelling storytelling, one of the most powerful tools in a sale's personal arsenal,

> *"If your story describes their problem better than they can describe it themselves, they will automatically assume you have got the best solution."*

But always remember to tell a story where your buyer is the main character, the problem he is facing is the villain, and your solution is the hero

4. Be an advisor

> *"78% of business buyers seek trusted advisors — not just salespeople — that add value to their business."*

SALESFORCE RESEARCH | STATE OF THE CONNECTED CUSTOMER

Remember this process of building pain by asking implication question (as shown in the example above) usually gives the buyers new insight on the problem differently than they perceived it to be, the buyer now needs to look at you as a trusted advisor because you can now see the problem through his perspective, and he considers you to be an expert advisor on this topic

It changes how your buyers think about the issue and once you have been able to establish trust your sale can push through faster,

Until this point your product positioning and your differentiation against your competitors will not matter much,

Here is an example of distinction once you have built the pain effectively

• "Your annual transaction is high, and you seem to get discounted rates from hotels as well."

• "However, the downside is that because you have consolidated your business to one /two hotels by contracting with them yearly, you still get a higher price on days the hotel rates go lower than your contracted rates."

• "If your KPI is to sustain cost, you seem to be paying more than 15% of your budget ."

We only introduce our key differentiator once the backstory is clear, and the buyer gets it. Then, our reps say something like this:

"Our Company provides a platform which does a real-time search optimization to present to you the lowest cost of the day; we check rates on multiple sources before offering to the client,"

Is it essential to lead to our differentiator and not with them? It just wouldn't land the same way if we started with the differentiator.

5. Customize presentation to the buyer

Your presentation should be speaking the buyer's language," Top salespeople realize that "in the corporate selling process, you are delegated to the person you sound like."

If you get too technical about the product, then you would be delegated to the professional or the operations team, if you are ROI driven, you would be appointed to head of procurement and finance, if you are too time, systems and implementation driven you will be delegated to the process manager,

E.g., "This is looking good to me.? Our EA to MD or Asst to Admin guy in charge of this kind of thing, you send me a mail, and I will connect you. "once he is convinced about your

offering, we can connect again."

While talking about your solution, use language reflecting on the issues faced by the buyer in front of you.

E.g., while you are selling to the C – Suite, you can speak more on a macro situation, along with issues that are more strategic and have profound implication,

And when you are talking to the user department or the junior level guys, you can build a conversation on the technical aspect this product solves.

6. Show the big picture first – Not the process

I have seen enthusiastic sellers getting so overwhelmed while describing their product that they get into every detail right from explaining the location from where the organization procures the raw material to how it transforms into the end product, they keep on speaking in length about how they maintain their quality/service, etc., I used to do that a lot myself until I realized that the client is not interested to know how we get to the solution of the problem in the initial presentation,

"But he is interested to know how the solution will look like once the entire sale is complete,"

During the presentation, you want to reveal an outcome/benefits of the final solution.

For example, if you are selling a software product, during your presentation, you can take them through a customized dashboard with company name and logo with its usability on how it will look and work,

Once he buys the idea, then you can break the presentation into parts on how every element of the dashboard will eventually be built.

7. SWOT Your competitors

When In hotels we used to do a SWOT (strength, weakness, opportunities, and threats) for top 5 competition hotels for the buyer,

Knowing our strengths and our competitor's vulnerability would allow us to position ourselves differently early in the presentation call,

For, eg.

What if you could show your buyer how your competitor's strengths make their product a poor fit?

When working with a service apartment chain, our job was to sell this apartment to the corporate companies in the vicinity.

Right across the road was a luxury 5* hotel rooms at a higher price than us, however many corporates chose to use that hotel instead of our service apartments, and they also paid higher for those rooms.

So, we did a SWOT of that hotel and learned that our competitor had the suite category of room, which was more significant than standard rooms, (but very surprising smaller than our smallest room) plus we had more amenities as well,

So, we positioned ourselves as an all-suite hotel where the client would get more than what he is getting at the luxury five* at a lesser price,

In no time we were regarded as the premium hotel, we sold more at a better price, and till date, this apartment gives its competitor hotels a run for their money.

Also, it's better to bring in the conversation of competitors SWOT earlier in the conversation rather than bringing it out during the price discussion; it puts you in much better control to get the outcome you want.

8. Building Urgency

In cognitive psychology and decision theory, people's tendency to prefer avoiding losses is more prominent than acquiring equivalent gains: this is known as the principal of loss aversion,

Here is an example to explain, if my current set up is making me a loss of 10 X value, I will focus on cutting the loss first then concentrate on other activities that can help me make the 10X value

If you highlight an active loss of revenue to the client, it builds urgency to act on a solution that protects loss

Every problem that the client is not working on can be demonstrated as a finical loss, for eg

Me – hi does your current set up gather booking data

Client – no our system can't do that, we make a manual report if required

Me – have you heard the principle that what cannot be measured, can never be controlled, can you share without capturing data, how would you be able to make MIS, without MIS how would you be able to know where the spending trends, and without knowing accurate spend trends how would you save money, based on the information you have given to me, I am comfortable in assuming that you would be losing at 10% of revenues due to non-data capturing

Once they have realized the potential loss, they will look up to the solutions you have to offer that helps them to stop losses; they will also use those points to differentiate your offerings in comparison to your competitors

9. Be cautious

While giving references- giving references to your clients is a great tool to build credibility but remember that it also can set you off as not in my league type of solution,

People relate to the tribe they belong, while giving a reference it's most important to speak about the same industry/division/nature of business they are into,

E.g., if I tell an automobile guy that we are working with Microsoft and they have some excellent testimonials for us, the buyer may think this kind of product is either expensive or not suitable for me,

And most important you need to share a relevant story about how the other company was facing a similar or more significant problem and how your product could solve those, Also sales superstars always build a tale starting with questions which seems like impossible to answer until your product enters, the stronger your story, the faster your close,

10. Discuss price after you establish value

If you speak on the price before demonstrating your products' solution, you can rest assured that you will not get the sale even if you are the lowest price in the market.

When buyers negotiate, they do not see the value of the price you are asking them to pay, on the contrary, the more significant value proposition you build and the more urgency you create, the more premium you can make.

So, always remember while setting the presentation's context, sellers can update their buyers that the pricing will come later in the presentation. I hope that is comfortable with all; you may note your pricing questions and ask us at the end of the presentation.

11. Ending your presentation well

Its where you finish that counts,

Sometimes sales presentations end in an untuned note such as That is all I have today. Would you have any questions please feel free to ask?" The salesperson is seen rushing through the end because the client is losing time and has to head out for the next meeting,

This section is to entice URGENCY AND MAKE THEM ACT, let's just say that a mighty close will be able to build up the same energy and enthusiasm which was at the start of the presentation which entices the client into some kind of advance or progress commitment,

Tell the story of where their business is now, and the vision of what it could be if they choose your offering. Making them look at their business problems differently is a way to differentiate against competitors.

Some exciting ways I have seen successful people close is

They reiterate the benefits of the solution and ask for the next step to action/commitment/ purchase etc.

They reiterate or repeat the answer to the most pressing objection raised by them,

My favorite is giving a compelling winning story which reiterates the most important product benefits and how our products and solutions have helped the other company and asking for a close

STORYTELLING

"After a presentation, 63% of attendees remember stories. Only 5% remember statistics." (Source: Chip and Dan Heath)

Now considering you and I are buyers and sellers, respectively, we happen to meet in your office. You ask me, so Rakesh, tell me what you do for a living, I give you two answers, you need to decide which one of the two are you most likely to remember.

Introduction 1

Hi, I take care of sales for a corporate hospitality solution provider, we manage all hospitality spends for corporations such as hotels, cars, and events.

Introduction 2

Before I introduce myself, let me share a quick experience with you.

Imaging its 7:30 pm on your regular workday, and your MD asks you to make some travel arrangements for him as he is visiting Bangalore at 3 am next day,

You quickly start reaching out to some cab vendors; confirm with one of them based on their availability and price. Simultaneously, you speak to 3 hotels to get your MD a room within his expected price range and in the closest vicinity to your client's office. By the time you complete managing this stuff, its 8 30 pm, and you reach home by 9:15 pm.

After a long day of work while you are fast asleep, at 2 am you get an unexpected call from the cab driver asking you, "madam, I can't find the location of pick up can you please explain in detail"?

The question here is how can we ease this booking process with the highest accuracy for our clients, as in the travel segment, there are a lot of moving parts, such as people and multiple companies who are involved in getting the guest from one location to another.

My organization is into providing a complete solution by joining these moving parts together (transport, hotels, and events) while improving efficiency and making it cost-effective in the process. I am responsible for managing the sales for this setup.

If your choice is the second option, congratulations you understand that storytelling can impact your audience,

Why is storytelling important?

"For people to buy your product they should remember your product when they need it," so it's surprising but true that the attention span of a human is 8 seconds, (even more surprisingly attention span of a goldfish is 9 seconds) all thanks to technology and the information we have access to our attention span has been reducing over the years;

Therefore, it becomes even more critical to capture your client's Mind Space so that they can remember to use your product when they need it.

People process information first with emotion and then with logic. Therefore, experts say that people remember stories 22 times more than remember facts and figures.

When do you use a story in a sales call?

Stories help a person to get an **emotional connection with a situation, person, brand, product, or any element almost instantly.**

You can use the story in any phase of the call.

E.g., if you want to build a connection with the client, use the story in the introduction phase.

Or, if you are going to build your brand credibility, you may use it in the presentation stage.

You can use a story in any phase of the call; the two most essential attributes of storytelling are 1) is **knowing** when to tell a story and 2) **choosing** the right story.

What are the elements of a good story?

1. **Hero is the main character**, usually a representation of the audience; they should be able to relate to him the best. E.g., **My client** XYZ company, had a leader in the automobile sector,

2. **Identification** – a situation where the hero, identifies that there is a need to change or transform the current situation

E.g., had challenges in managing their hotel accommodation and transport arrangement for employees.

3. **Challenge** – a case where the hero faces multiple problems

E.g., they had a booking process with only 3 - 4 hours of booking window, if their travel management team missed out or got delayed to action emails, which happened quite often, their employees had to pay extra for tickets. Their travel teams were reactive to the situation, and finance teams were always shelling out more money on cancellations and amendments.

4. **Doctor**- That is where you enter with a solution to the problem, make sure you explain the solution in detail.

E.g., After hearing them out, we realized that it was not only a costing issue they were facing, but the personal credibility of the HR and travel team was at stake. Because both these departments were responsible for travel, any lapse on their vendor part impacting the employees travel routine showed them in poor light.

We provided them a tool, which gave power and control back to the company; the employees use this tool directly to make the bookings. Therefore the admin and services team can focus on more urgent tasks and management.

Sending automated confirmation and immediately raising invoices along with MIS and other reports was one of the key highlights of this technology. Here is a testimonial from our client.

5. **Emotion** – The binding thread of the entire story is emotion, and if your story can demonstrate that it had a positive impact on people who were a part of the outcome, it is more likely to resonate with the client.

E.g., when we presented our solution to the client, they thought that once we have our technology in place, their travel team guys may not be required in the company anymore. Today both the travel guys are happy and a part of the HR team managing internal employee engagement.

Have a Story bank

Critical elements of your story are **its authenticity, and its relevance** to the situation. If your story is non-authentic, your buyers will understand and may lose trust early in the sales cycle, and if your story is non-relevant to the location, the buyer may get disengage very quickly.

Storytelling can be used at all places, while the introduction stage, problem-solving stage, rapport building rapport, or even while presenting.

Therefore, to have so many multiple authentic stories, it is imperative to have a story bank that can be shared between you and your colleagues.

And lastly, like all other skills, **great storytelling becomes better with practice,** so go ahead and keep practicing this great skill until the world speaks about your story one day.

REFERRAL

Referrals are known to be the most effective forms of advertisement; references encompass both the pillars of selling.

1) It builds trust for the seller.

2) Its builds credibility for the seller

"84% of buyers start their buying process from a referral. (Harvard Business Review)"

"92% of buyers trust product/service referrals from those they know. (Nielsen)"

Besides **saving energy** in finding and moving up the sales cycle with the right customer, referrals also build in a **social pressure to buy the product.**

Another advantage is that if your existing user has personally advocated for your product, **you get less resistance** from your client. Your selling cycle becomes shorter, and you see quick results.

Most importantly, referred clients often **spend more on their initial purchase with you, resulting in better profits.**

Remember, with referrals, you will most likely be **connected to the right customer** because the user of your product or service will refer you to a person who exactly needs your product or service. More because of a peer to peer industry connect.

When referrals can directly save time, effort, and help you make more money why is it that most sellers do not use this method, let us look at some facts in the following section

Why sellers do not refer

Non-referral comes from a varied belief system,

• Some do not want to sound or appear too desperate for work; it makes them extremely uncomfortable asking their customers for a referral.

• Some are not sure if their products are delivering value to the client that they can ask about referrals.

• Individual salespeople also feel that it may put the relationship with the client in an uncomfortable situation, or they may get perceived as being needy or pushy.

• Some fear rejection

• Some people think referrals should happen naturally

• Many salespeople do not think of a reference as an impactful sale generator.

I have only one response to all these belief systems, *"you are hurting your selling potential by not asking for referrals."*

> *You may never lose business by asking for business, but if you do not ask for it, you will surely lose a lot.*

> *In a research conducted by Texas Tech, you will be happy to know that 83% of customers are glad to give a referral after a positive experience.*

Unfortunately, only 29% do, because salespeople don't ask.

But before you get started, make sure you are doing the following:

Be referable. It would be best if you came beyond the selling; you need to ensure that you have been able to deliver what you have promised, and the **client finds value working with you.** Therefore, to deliver more value to your client,

• **Be responsive** – Make sure you are staying on top of things. If you are ready to demonstrate flexibility and sympathy, then clients will reciprocate accordingly.

• **Be sincere** – your sincerity towards a client influences their commitment towards you, therefore find your balance and be in every activity you perform in dealing with them.

• **Be consistent** – Building credibility needs consistency in approach, clients are human, and they observe changes in behavior; therefore, always be consistent in your plan.

Who should I ask for a referral?

Leverage your entire network as you do not know where the gold is hidden,

First, start by asking your Advocates – those who are happy with your service, share a good bond with you and will be glad to talk you up appropriately. They will connect you with the most appropriate target market.

Secondly you can take references from industry connections, former and present colleagues, friends, and family, etc. However, they may be a more broad-based connection because they have not used your products and are providing references on the relationship you share with them.

When should I ask for a referral?

There are multiple schools of thought on this topic; some experts recommend asking for a referral as soon as you close the deal because the client is convinced about our services as he has bought our product,

Others suggest that we should only ask for referrals once the client has used our product satisfactorily; my only concern is that we might lose on an opportunity to serve in a fast-paced world if we wait that long.

I recommend two steps.

Step 1 - Seeding – Whenever in a sales cycle your relationship demonstrates, open communication, trustworthiness, and Likability, you can plant the seed of referral to your client, you can mention like

"Hi Abhishek, I need your support; once I can demonstrate our solution to your best use and are completely satisfied with our service/delivery, please refer me to someone you think would benefit from our services." I hope that's comfortable with you.

Step 2 - Deliver Value - Before asking for a referral, always earn the right to do so, and that will only happen once your client sees value in your commitment, delivery, and service. Walk the extra mile to deliver value; this way, you will always earn your referral.

Your cue to value delivery will be when you receive and appreciation from the client; **this is the most effective time for earning your referral.**

Here is a 6-step framework to ask for referrals

1) **Get Specific** – What you are looking for is an introduction to a new client, with a recommendation about how well your products/services solve common problems faced by them.

However, when a salesperson asks general referral questions like, "can you connect me to someone you think needs my product "?

The client interprets this as "I think he is just looking for names and numbers of some people "

General question will get you a general response, therefore, it essential to be as specific as possible to your requirements like

Here is an example: "I'm looking to be connected with travel heads/HR heads from automation companies based in Pune, who are looking to streamline their hospitality spends."

Else you can also reach for an exact profile you want and ask.

On your LinkedIn, you are connected with Mr. XYZ from ABC company; we have a great solution. Can you link us and put the right word about us to them.

2) Make it simple - Do the work for your referrer and send him a forwardable email template that he can send to his peer network.

3) Always follow up – Once you send an email, make sure your follow up to generate response. In case you have already had a meeting with the person referred to, do demonstrates equal pro-activeness and sincerity in dealing with the client.

4) Create a networking platform - Host your clients for a net-working meal where they can invite their referral partner as well,

This strategy is the absolute best approach for attracting new clients. By encouraging both clients and prospects, you will see your clients begin selling for you.

5) Express Gratitude - It may seem as a general point. Still, its effectiveness is extremely high; this is good advice in life, period. Always show gratitude when someone does something beautiful for you. Incentivizing referrals or not, but do thank your customers for their help.

6) Give a Referral – Givers always gain salespeople who connect their clients to their network partners and receive more referrals than others.

In conclusion, I would like to reiterate that Perseverance and Patience will be your best friends to help you get maximum results

Create a referral System

Referrals need to become part of your sales culture, therefore always ask for referrals on the phone, through email, during demos, etc.

Ask for one introduction per day, this might sound like a lot of work, but how long does it take to ask for a single introduction? You should be able to accomplish this in just 15 minutes -- so make it the most important 15 minutes of your day, every workday.

If you do this activity for one year, you could get up to 200 new referrals a year and that a lot of leads.

Start Today:

If you have not embraced a referral culture, start embracing it! Asking for referrals is something that you can start doing today. Look at where you have your best relationships.

EPILOGUE

Groan Kropp, a mountaineer and adventurer, left Stockholm on 16 October 1995, on a specially designed bicycle with 108 kilograms.

He traveled 13,000 kilometers to arrive at Everest Base Camp, this expedition took him 6 + months (April 1996).

Three weeks later, on 23 May, he tackled the mountain, successfully summitting **without extra oxygen support and the help of a sherpa**. He then cycled part of the way back home.

So, the question we want to answer is that was this **expedition challenging or was it impossible,**

Connecting it back to our sales lives, some clients, some budget, and some tasks may be challenging, but if we make up our mind to accomplish it, its neve impossible. All we need to do is take action to change it.

> *"It is not because things are difficult that we do not dare; it is because we do not dare that they are difficult."*

Seneca

I want to leave you with a final thought *"Every sales champion of today was an ordinary sales guy of yesterday. They took action to put in the EXTRA effort, which makes them Extraordinary.*

In sales, your result for tomorrow is the reward of the effort you put in yesterday, therefore, to enjoy a better tomorrow, take charge, and act today.

I wish you all the best in your career.

ABOUT THE AUTHOR

Rakesh Lalchandani

With the belief that sales is a skill that can be mastered by everyone, Rakesh has set out on his path to identify and share these learnable traits demonstrated by successful salespeople today.

With over 12 years in B2B selling, he has used these principles for personal growth and achieve success in his career. He wants this knowledge to be shared to help sales leaders of tomorrow.

Born raised in Pune, he started his selling journey as a retail salesperson at the age of 18 and then moved onto telesales in a call center. Today, with over 10 + years in hospitality sales, and an entrepreneur at heart, he continually seeks to upgrade himself and his surroundings by challenging the status quo.

WHAT WILL YOU GET

Whether you are starting your corporate sales journey or are looking at refreshing your selling skills, with the application of techniques mentioned in this book you will be able to upgrade your sales career

Sales is a mental sport, and the difference between top performers and average performers is that high performers are moving scared and average performer frozen stiff.

This book will give you bite-sized action steps to build your sales, through this book you can learn,

5S method Lean Management used for personal effectiveness in selling,

Use the AIDA method of high influence presentation to the client.

Learn how to keep your pipeline full of genuine prospects.

Perfect the telephone skills and getting face-to-face with your buyer.

Build your 30sec sales pitch to create an impactful first impression.

Learn how to generate more leads from your current clients through the art of referrals.

Learn to use stories to sell effectively.

www.ingramcontent.com/pod-product-compliance
Lightning Source LLC
Chambersburg PA
CBHW051243160726
47994CB00003B/1007